ST AGNES

A PHOTOGRAPHIC HISTORY

VOLUME TWO

VILLAGE & SHOPS

CLIVE BENNEY

WHEAL HAWKE
PUBLICATIONS

Foreword

This book, the second in a series about St Agnes, takes a look at the
village and shops from Penwinnick Road through Vicarage Road and
Churchtown to Town Hill. It was not my intention to write a history of
every shop and building but to concentrate more on the many changes that
have taken place over the years including the disappearance of many
businesses and buildings of note.

With the increase in mining activity in the 18th and 19th centuries
St Agnes grew rapidly and Churchtown expanded to become the
commercial and social centre of the village with its new hotels, shops
and market. Trade directories of this period list many services and shops
which have long ceased to exist including a hatter, watch and clock maker,
saddler, tinplate worker, grate manufacturer and druggist.

I am indebted to Tom Thompson and Frank Carpenter, two of my
predecessors as recorders of the St Agnes Old Cornwall Society. In the late
1970s and early 1980s they interviewed and recorded the reminiscences of
many older residents of the village. Frank also carried out extensive
research in trade directories, village guides and church magazines which he
used in his book, *The Story of a Village Street*, in which he lists the history of
the shops and buildings in the main street from 1900 to 1985.

I have continued this research by interviewing additional people and by
extracting information from old newspapers, trade directories and other
documents to add first hand information about some of the incidents that
have taken place in the village. I have also included a vast number of
previously unpublished photographs and I hope that the resultant book
will appeal not only to those who grew up in the community but also to
newcomers and the younger generation who would like to learn more
about the history of our village.

Clive Benney 2006

First published in 2006 by
Wheal Hawke Publications:

14 Trevaunance Road
St Agnes
Cornwall
TR5 0SE

Design by Daniel Benney
www.danielbenney.co.uk

ISBN 0-9550510-1-0

Printed by:
R Booth Ltd
Antron Hill
Mabe
Penryn

Contents

St Agnes From the Beacon c. 1905

Beacon Garage

left The petrol pumps and wooden kiosk during the early days of the garage.

We begin our look at the village with Peterville and Dale's Garage in Penwinnick Road. Until 1990 this garage was called Beacon Garage, a strange name considering its distance from the Beacon.

After the Second World War Will Thomas started work as a mechanic for Bill Dale at Dale's Garage, St Agnes. Will had learnt his trade at West Cornwall Motors and H T P Motors at Truro; during the war he had worked for Westland Aircraft in Yeovil. Sometime around 1948 Will left Dale's to start his own garage at Cannonball Farm, Beacon Road, St Agnes. This had been the Thomas' family home where Will had grown up; it was then occupied by his brother, Bert, and wife Annie.

Will used two buildings adjoining the road; one had double doors and an inspection pit and the other was the workshop with a bench. He named it Beacon Garage.

In the early 1950s the site of the present garage in Penwinnick Road was cleared for the owner, Mr Jarmen. It consisted of the ruins of an old cottage or cottages adjoining the road and some mine waste at the rear. Percy Cheesley undertook the clearance work; he was employed by R S Jose of Truro. He remembers driving a bulldozer to push the rubble to the rear of the site. The only thing taken away was the roadside hedging stone.

Shortly after, Will bought the site and erected petrol pumps and a small kiosk. At first Will's wife, Avis, served petrol with only the kiosk for shelter and warmth; meanwhile Will continued to work at Cannonball Farm.

The pumps were powered by a generator in a shed at the rear of the site and Will's son, Alan, remembers that he and his brother had to start the engine on their way to school.

Eventually, at the end of 1955, Alan and Donald Mitchell built a new garage on the site and Will moved there from the Beacon site taking the name Beacon Garage with him. Three new pumps were installed and an electric supply brought in from Presingoll Farm.

Alan Thomas worked with his parents at the garage and, in addition to selling petrol and carrying out vehicle maintenance, they had a Morris agency supplying new cars. This later changed to BMC (British Motor Corporation) and then BLMC (British Leyland Motor Corporation).

In 1972 the garage was sold to Anne and Rick Robinson who sold it to Geoff Williams in 1987. In 1990 it was bought by the present owner Keith Woolcott who then changed the name from Beacon Garage to Peterville and Dales Garage.

top Will Thomas standing
beside the petrol pumps
in front of the new
garage.

above Beacon Garage in
the 1960s

Penwinnick Road

above This 1920s postcard has the title "Station Road, St Agnes" and shows a narrow road leaving the village and heading towards the St Agnes Railway Station near Presingoll Farm. The station was a part of the Chacewater to Newquay branch line and served the village from 1903 until the line closure in 1963. Because of the contours of the land the station was almost a mile from the village it served and over the years many people walked this road carrying their heavy suitcases.

right Penwinnick Road, outside Penkerris, in 1985 and before the building of Penwinnick Close. The road was very narrow at this point with overhanging trees; many people will remember clearing branches from the road after a winter storm.

top Penwinnick Road 1977 before the grass verge was laid and the barn converted to a dwelling. *Photo Tom Thompson*

above Penwinnick Road in 2006.

The Museum

St Agnes Museum took its first steps in October 1983, when a group of friends discussed the possibility of establishing a small parish museum in Thomas' Engine House - close to the main street of St Agnes. Unfortunately planning problems prevented this happening.

However, the seed was sown and the idea of a museum began to appeal to many local people; a constitution was drafted and the search for a building began.

In the meantime a catalogue of exhibits was started and many new and interesting artefacts came to light and were displayed at exhibitions. Work was also undertaken to preserve the Wheal Trevaunance winding engine site at Higher Bal.

Eventually a temporary museum site was found at Peterville - where Saffron Gallery used to be. The museum knew that this would be a temporary home but it was a start and on the 22nd July 1986 Ron Simmons performed the official opening.

The museum had some very successful years there but in 1989 they acquired the present site - the old chapel of rest in Penwinnick Road. At their meeting in January of that year the Parish Council granted the Museum Trust a 25-year lease. However, much work and fundraising was needed before the museum could open to the public. The work fell into two broad categories (1) the connection of mains water and electricity to the building and the installation of a septic tank and (2) the construction of a first floor and the installation of wiring, heating, and fixtures and fittings to achieve the required layout.

On Saturday the 4th April 1992 Alice Bizley - the wife of the author of *Friendly Retreat* - officially opened the new museum. (Mrs Bizley was an artist and illustrated the book on the parish) About eighty guests attended the event.

Since then St Agnes Museum has gone from strength to strength with excellent visitor numbers and new exhibits and displays each year.

above The opening of the museum in 1992. Mrs Alice Bizley cuts the ribbon with Chairman John Sawle (right) and Secretary Roger Radcliffe.

top, right The Museum's giant Leatherback Turtle. Its dead body was washed up on Porthtowan Beach in September 1988; it is believed to have been 80 years old.

Right The Lady Agnes Figurehead.

far right St Agnes Museum 2006.

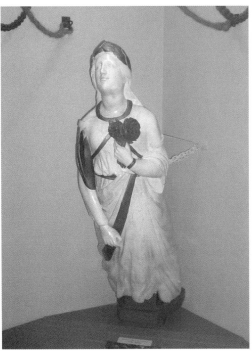

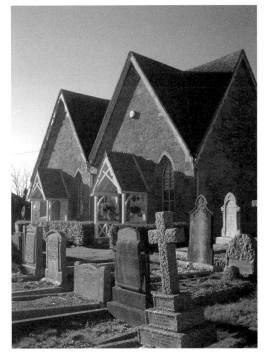

Dale's Garage

below Garage staff c. 1940 - Alf Bunt, Bill Dyer, Selwyn Magor and Bill Dale.

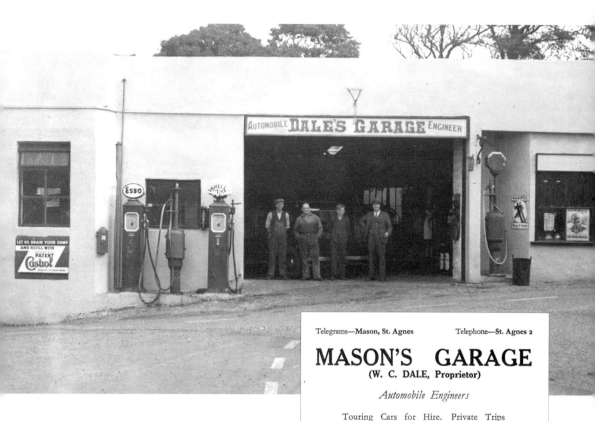

below Garage staff c. 1940 - Alf Bunt, Bill Dyer, Selwyn Magor and Bill Dale.

Telegrams—Mason, St. Agnes   Telephone—St. Agnes 2

MASON'S   GARAGE
(W. C. DALE, Proprietor)

Automobile Engineers

Touring Cars for Hire. Private Trips Arranged. Regular Market Services. Best Class Tyres Always Stocked. Vacuum Oils. Motor and Cycle Accessories. Any Make of Car Supplied.

ST. AGNES · · · · · CORNWALL

At the top of Vicarage Road, by the roundabout, there is house called Dales Yard. This house was built on the site of a garage known to most people as Dale's Garage. The late Alf Bunt, born in 1904, in a taped interview with Frank Carpenter in 1983, remembered the area from when he was a boy. *"Well, there used to be a coal shed there when I was boy and then Mason and Gripe had it as a garage. Mr Gripe used to be one of the old members of St Agnes and Mr Mason came here after the war. They went into partnership in the motor business, Gripe was the electrician and Mason the driver and mechanic. They sold the garage to Bill Dale, it was half the size it became later. Bill Dale dropped the front wall and brought it out to the road and he did a nice job of it."*

Alf was later employed by Bill Dale as a mechanic but he was also a blacksmith and worked for a time with Johnny Murrish. Johnny remembers that access to the blacksmith shop was through an opening to the right of the garage in the lane that led to Rosemundy House. John Dale, Bill's son, remembers it from when he was a boy, *"This was a mysterious place, sometimes full of smells and heat. This was the forge. Beside the entrance was a bench, which was always covered with tools. There was plenty of grease and oil and often cars, which needed to be repaired. They were driven over a Stygian 'pit' in which they were examined from below with the help of a special torch. I don't remember the men who worked there in the early days but I recall Frank Williams, Frank Fiddick, John Murrish, Selwyn Magor, Bill Dyer and Alf Bunt. I remember at times we had a Dodge and a Buick and, before that, a Vauxhall. Most cars were black and I recall the AA men saluting my father, as they did to*

all members of the Association at that time. *As a garage proprietor my father was among the first subscribers to the telephone directory and our number was St Agnes 2. In 1948 it changed to St Agnes 302.*"

From 1966 to 1973 the garage was run by Mr Grounds and from 1973 until its closure, in 1990, by the Woolcott Family.

top .A car fills with petrol outside the garage in the 1940's

above Demolition of the garage in 1994

Goonvrea Road

GOONVREA RD, ST. AGNES.

Until the late 1930s three very pretty, white-washed, thatched cottages nestled at the bottom of Goonvrea Road. Unfortunately, as is the case with many other properties in this book, two were destroyed by fire.

The author has been unable to find any newspaper references to these fires but they must have been fierce and, with the thatch well alight, destruction was quick. There was not much to save by the time the fire brigade arrived from Truro or Redruth.

top Cottage at the bottom of Goonvrea Road destroyed by fire in the 1930s.

above The bottom of Goonvrea Road in 1985.

Dale's Corner and 4 & 5 Vicarage Road

This view shows the top of Vicarage Road c. 1925. Just to the right of centre is the old cottage that stood on the site of the present day fish shop. Alf Bunt remembered the cottage from when he was a boy, "*I used to go up there. It was owned by a fellow by the name of Percy Trethewey, he used to cut the boys' hair and generally clean them up a bit. Percy used scissors, comb and horse clippers - we used to come out shades lighter.*"

Percy Trethewey drove a horse bus and later, the first St Agnes motor bus - a model "T" Ford with open sides. He did his hair cutting in his spare time.

When Bill Dale took over the garage next door the purchase also included this cottage. As part of the alterations to the garage he had the cottage demolished and the present shop with accommodation above, erected; it sold confectionery and tobacco.

The white building to the right, on the corner with Polbreen Lane, was a lock-up shop with no living accommodation. At this time it was used for boot and shoe repairs. Before then Mr Westlake travelled from Truro to run a saddler and general leatherwork shop there.

above Bill Dale's new shop c. 1940

In 1926 Sidney Herbert Richards purchased the building and the adjoining small cottage; he demolished both and built the present day shop and flat above.

left The shop, cottage and lock-up in 1909.

left No. 4 Vicarage Road. This shop dates back to at least the 1870s when it was a tobacconist, sweet and toyshop owned by Mrs Sarah Blackney. Alf Bunt remembered going into the shop to buy rolled tobacco and being given a free clay pipe to smoke. Around 1923 Thomas Edward Dunstan used the building as his first chemist shop in St Agnes.

When this picture was taken in January 1977 it sold sweets, ice cream and a few electrical goods; Mrs Borlase ran it. She was a delightful lady who loved children coming into her shop to chat and to taste her delicious ice cream. In fact if you kept her talking she continued to fill the cone with her wooden spoon until it was piled high. She retired in 1977, aged 93. Her friends knew her as Minty and when the shop was converted to a dwelling, sometime around 1978; it was given the name Minty's Cottage.
Photo Tom Thompson

65 Vicarage Road

For many years the thatched building in the centre of the view was a pork butcher's shop with a dwelling house attached. On the 23rd October 1908 a disastrous fire destroyed the building, furniture and stock; at that time Fred James occupied it. A few days later the Royal Cornwall Gazette (RCG) reported, "*Mr James who retired about midnight was aroused at 1.20am by his wife and they found the house full of smoke and the roof above the stairs well alight. Hastily putting on a few items of clothing they caught up their children and carried them across the street to Mrs Gregory's who took care of them. Several of the neighbours, together with PC Benney, tried to get into the bedrooms in order to save some of the furniture etc. but without avail. The stairs soon gave way, and then the ceiling fell with a thud only about ten minutes after the family had left the room. The fire by this time had reached some pails of lard, and this burnt fiercely, the flames shooting up to a great height. The burning thatch was blown across the street but no damage was done.*

The house and stock were completely burnt, nothing now standing but the bare walls and these are crumbling as the wood lintels are being burnt out. The origin of the fire is unknown."

At the Parish Council meeting the following week the fire was discussed and the need for a fire hose. It was pointed out that there was one available but hardly anyone knew about it. The RCG stated "*...there was a hose 60 foot long in the custody of Mr M G Roberts, the engineer of the waterworks and in cases of emergency an application to his residence will ensure the loan of the hose, which possibly might save a serious conflagration. The council will consider getting further lengths of hose at the next meeting. A suggestion was thrown out for the formation of a volunteer fire brigade with an occasional drill.*"

The house was rebuilt the following year as a two storey, stone building with a tiled roof. In 1936 Sidney Herbert Richards moved from his newsagent's shop across the road to this house and became a fruiterer and greengrocer. The first

thing he did was to replace the left hand front room window with a shop bay window.

When Tommy Coombe moved into the house in the early 1980s he found the old front window in the garden shed. He put it back to replace the shop window. The house was then as it was when first built.

top The remains of the building after the fire.

above Postmarked 1910 this postcard shows 65 and 66 Vicarage Road after rebuilding.

Vicarage Road

C.1912 - this view shows boys and girls posing for the photographer while the postman on the left takes no notice and continues to empty the pillar box, his hand-pulled cart beside him. The pillar box stood here until it was moved to the corner of Rosemundy Hill, adjacent to the old mortuary.

Behind him, on the corner, is a grocery and drapery shop run by Hannah Stribley. Alf Bunt said, "*She sold everything from a yard of elastic to a tin of biscuits*". More recently the shop has been a tobacconist, confectionery, sports and finally, before conversion into part of the dwelling house, a gift shop - Choices.

At this time the shop to the left was a pork butcher's but it later became, and remained for many years, a grocery, confectionery and tobacconist shop. By the 1930s a lean-to structure had been added to the end to create a larger shop but this was later replaced with a more permanent single storey building. Sometime around 1962 the shop owner, Clyde Bartle, had it converted to two storeys with the shop below and living accommodation above.

In 1965 Clyde Bartle had a new shop built in the garden next door (where the white wall is in this view) and transferred his grocery and provision side of the business there.

Today the original shop is C P and S News and the newer shop is a Spar grocery.

above c.1955

9 Vicarage Road

When this photo was taken c. 1910 most of the shops at this end of Vicarage Road were on the opposite side to today. There was a variety of shops there - a tailor, a newsagent and tobacconist, a grocery/sweet shop and a dairy.

By 1940 all but one had become residential; the only remaining shop was No. 9 - the one on the right. This continued as a fruit and greengrocery shop until 1978. In that year the gable end collapsed and the occupiers, Mr and Mrs Tre Smith, had to leave in a hurry. The rubble fell into Vicarage Road and the entrance to the Railway Inn car park.

The newspaper reported, *"Carrick Council inspected the damage and served a dangerous structure notice on the owners, Devenish (Redruth) Brewery Ltd who sent in the demolition men. The Brewery Managing Director said they would be making the site as tidy as they could to prevent it becoming an eyesore."*

Within 24 hours the house had been demolished and today the site is the Railway Inn beer garden.

above 1st January 1977.
Photo Tom Thompson.

above No.9 Vicarage Road in 1978 showing the collapsed gable end.

left Demolition in progress.

55 & 56 Vicarage Road

A lovely sunny day c. 1910 in Vicarage Road. A young boy with a pick over his shoulder poses outside the Smiths Arms and Railway Hotel. S J Govier, a photographer from Chacewater, took the photograph. The building on the left, No. 55, where the village chemist is today, looks very different. At this time it was a tobacconist, fancy dealer, bakery and refreshment house run by Samuel John Hooper and the entrance to the shop was on the side - at the top of Rosemundy Hill. Early postcards also show a flat roofed shop attached to the side of the building also belonging to Mr Hooper. It was not until Mr Dunstan moved into these premises in 1927 that the side entrance was bricked up and a new front entrance formed adjacent to No. 56 in Vicarage Road.

above Major alterations were undertaken with large shop windows installed to Nos. 55 (chemist) and 56 (general drapers run by Mr S J Williams).
In 1978 both shops were combined into one property. Today it's the village chemist.

top No. 56 Vicarage Road
in the 1960s when it was
the Radio House run by
Frederick Olds - radio,
camera and ciné specialist.

above c. 1908 St Agnes
band lead a procession
past Mr Hooper's flat
roofed shop at the top
of Rosemundy Hill.

The Railway Inn

The Railway Inn has catered for the needs of the inhabitants of St Agnes for over 150 years. The first recorded landlord was Thomas Tregellas - listed in Salter's Trade Directory of Cornwall of 1852/53. Eight years earlier Pigot's Directory (1844) does not list the Inn although it does list nine other public houses in St Agnes.

In 1856 Thomas Tregellas was recorded as the licensee of the Smiths Arms and also as the local blacksmith - his workshop was on the opposite side of the road. The original name of the pub, Smiths Arms, probably came from this time when Thomas held both positions. When he died in 1862 he was buried in the Old Burial Ground in a grave opposite the pub and within six feet of his old blacksmith's shop.

Various licensees followed and in 1908 it was John Hawkey who changed the name to the Smiths Arms and Railway Hotel - the Chacewater to Newquay railway branch line having come to St Agnes five years earlier.

It wasn't until the 1920s that it became the Railway Inn.

top A long name board above the pub c. 1910 to accommodate the words Smiths Arms and Railway Hotel.

above L-R Bob Gay, Gerry Jones, Malcolm Pearson and Donald Tremain outside the Railway Inn July 1985.

The Mortuary

above c.1982 demolition of the wall beside the old mortuary to build seating area.

top The old mortuary shortly after the end wall had been taken out, showing the old and new letterboxes.

On the corner of Rosemundy Hill and Vicarage Road there is a small building through which there is pedestrian access to the old cemetery - now the Garden of Rest. Wooden benches placed inside offer people the opportunity to sit and relax.

The building was erected in the early 1800s as the village mortuary and used for well over a hundred years. For the majority of this time it didn't even have basic facilities like water and drainage; water had to be obtained from a standpipe on the pavement outside.

Dr Henry Whitworth saw his first post-mortem at this mortuary in the late 1930s; his father Dr Cuthbert Whitworth carried it out by the light of a hurricane lamp. By the time Dr Henry (Whitworth) came to practice in St Agnes, in 1946, the mortuary had closed.

Douglas Mitchell of Goonown remembers driving the old Morris gate-change St John's ambulance to the pedestrian entrance of the old cemetery (where the letter box is in the wall today). He said, *"We had to unload the body in the road and Dr Cuthbert Whitworth, Cuthy we called him, would not allow us in until after dark when he would be waiting inside with his oil lamp to do what he had to do"*. Douglas thinks his last delivery was just after the Second World War.

The building was boarded up after closure but used for a couple of years between 1954 and 1956 as a club room for the newly formed St Agnes Surf Life Saving Club - the mortuary slab being used as a table.

In the middle to late 1960s Brian Trickett was employed by the Parish Council to convert the building into the lych-gate of today. Inside, behind a rickety old door, he found the slate slab and a butler sink. The wall on the roadside was solid and Brian had to create a new arch to the entrance. Unfortunately it was obstructed by a large pillar box which had been moved from further up the road. Brian was paid a further seven shillings and six pence (37½P) to build up the old entrance to the cemetery, between the two granite gateposts, and to build in a new letterbox. The old pillar box was then removed.

Rosemundy Hill

A view of the cottages that once stood at the top of Rosemundy Hill c.1890.

Constructed with cob walls and thatched roofs there was no access to them from the Rosemundy Hill side - the entrances were at the rear. Sometime around 1900 the cottages were demolished and replaced by a row of four stone - built houses with slate roofs.

right Hooper and Son's Baker's delivery wagon in 1906.

left Rosemundy Hill c. 1905. This postcard is postmarked May 1905 and was sent to the author's great aunt, Ethel Benney, at the police house in British Road where her father was the village policeman. Later, one of the houses in Rosemundy Hill became the village police house.

left Houses in Rosemundy Hill c. 1910

left A view up Rosemundy Hill c. 1900

The Village Blacksmith

below The blacksmith at work c. 1905.

A Trade Directory of 1856 records Thomas Tregellas as the Blacksmith in Vicarage, St Agnes, and also as the licensee of the Smiths Arms. The next recorded blacksmith in Kelly's Directory of Cornwall is Thomas's son, George, in 1873. Frank Carpenter's research shows that Thomas was the blacksmith from c. 1840 to c. 1856 and George from c. 1873 up to his death in 1898, when he was aged 66 years.

Reminiscing for the St Agnes Women's Institute album of 1951 Mr Lawrence remembered George at work. "*I wish I could show you a mental picture that I have as once seen in Vicarage Road, the old-time smithy looking up the street from where Dockings shop now stands, the smith sturdy and strong, with massive arms, and shapely head and beard, the very image of his craft. And now his name is found in the old cemetery, about six feet from his old forge - George Tregellas.*"

George was buried in the family grave with his father, Thomas; the headstone is still visible today.

The blacksmith's was where the shop Inspired Earth is today. Work ceased there before the First World War and Frederick John Gribben bought the derelict remains of the building. His name appears in the 1914 edition of Kelly's Trade Directory as a cycle agent in Vicarage Road. It was later used as an ironmongery shop and as a hairdresser's.

Fred Gribben remained there up to 1946 when the shop was taken over by Fred Docking as a general china, glass and hardware store; he left in 1973.

above A very early view of Vicarage Road c. 1895. Unfortunately the blacksmith's shop is just out of view on the left. However the man on the right with apron and beard is blacksmith George Tregellas.

left The Handyman shop in 1985.

Spargo's Shop

This 1905 photograph shows three cottages which have now either gone or been altered beyond recognition. Behind the man in the white jacket, Tom Benney, is a white cottage with a garden - at right angles to the road. To the right are two more cottages, Nos. 15 and 16, which were demolished in 1959 when Trelawney Road was constructed to allow access to the new council houses.

At this time the white cottage was residential but in the mid 1930s Mark Uglow converted the property and moved there from his gentlemen's outfitters shop in Churchtown. It was then a single storey, flat roofed shop in the garden facing the road.

In the late 1950s and 1960s the shop was called Spargo's Drapers and Outfitters and from 1968 to its closure in 1995 David and Stella Tiddy were the proprietors.

In 1997 it was demolished and a new shop built; it is now occupied by Miller Countrywide Estate Agents.

above David and Stella Tiddy in the doorway of their shop in 1994. Although they ran the shop for many years they retained the name Spargo - seen here above the window.

right Millers Countrywide Estate Agent's offices in 2006. To the left is a small fruit and greengrocery shop. Alf Bunt remembered the building as a cottage, "*The front of the old cottage was torn down and a chip shop put in, a fellow by the name of Stone ran it*".

below Demolition of the
old shop in 1997.

15 & 16
Vicarage Road

Numbers 15 and 16 Vicarage Road were two cottages that were demolished in 1959 to provide space for the building of Trelawney Road leading to the new council houses. By the side of No. 16 was a lane that led to the fields at the back of the village. Alf Bunt remembered a slaughterhouse in the lane - it was used by the butcher, Bill Harris.

On the other side of the lane, in Vicarage Road, was Lloyds Bank Ltd. At the time of demolition both cottages were residential. In the early 1900s the room on the left of No. 16 was used by Miss Mary Stephens as a sweet shop. She was a favourite with the children selling Tom Trot sweets with peppermint flavouring. She also made and sold Cornish pasties. Vi Paull gave the author a copy of her Tom Trot sweet recipe:

"1lb treacle, 1lb moist sugar, ¼ lb butter, a few drops of essence of peppermint.

Have a saucepan large enough to allow a fast boiling over a clear fire. Put in the butter, rubbing it well over the bottom of the pan. Then add the sugar, treacle and peppermint, stirring gently with a knife. When it has boiled for 10 minutes drop a little off the knife into basin of cold water, when sufficiently done it will be crisp.

If not brittle, boil a little longer. Butter thoroughly or oil a shallow tin and into this pour the toffee, when beginning to set, mark it out into squares to make it easier to divide when cold. This recipe will make about 2lbs of toffee."

From c. 1926 until its demolition, No. 16 was the home of the village undertaker, firstly Matthew Hodge followed by Mark Hellyer.

top A band marches down Vicarage Road beside Nos. 15 and 16. A rare view of these now demolished cottages.

above A snowy day and the milk is being delivered by tractor and trailer. Behind is the wall at the end of No. 16, the lane and Lloyds Bank.

above Butcher Bill Harris carries a dead pig over his shoulder outside what is believed to be his slaughterhouse c. 1910.

top Vicarage Road at its junction with Trelawney Road in 2006.

The Men's Institute

The original Institute was established in 1841 and was located in Churchtown but after about 30 years the organisation ceased. Dr William Whitworth resurrected it in 1882.

In 1889 a letter was received from John Passmore Edwards who offered to present the institute with 200 books. It was in this year that he began his generous donations of public buildings with the construction of an Institute for Blackwater.

Dr Whitworth continued negotiations with him until a communication was received in which he expressed a desire to build and present to the town of St Agnes, a public reading room and library.

On the 16th March 1893 John Passmore Edwards purchased a plot of land from Francis G Enys, one of the main landowners in St Agnes. It

was a section of a large field which had been partly developed in 1881 by the construction of the Oddfellows Hall (now the Meadery). On the 28th June 1893 the land and the completed building were conveyed by deed of gift to trustees for use, "*In perpetuity, for literary and scientific purposes as an institute or reading room for the public benefit and to be known as the Miners and Mechanics Institute*".

right The Institute in 1992 when the wall and railings were moved back five feet to allow the construction of a pavement.

above Everyone in the street stops for the photographer c. 1905, even the two men on the donkey shay. Lloyds Bank's ornate railings and gate are to the left, next to those of the Miners and Mechanics Institute. This was the only building in Vicarage Road and Churchtown to retain its railings during the Second World War because it was used as a school for evacuees.

The Village Cobbler

below William Butcher stands in the doorway of his shop c. 1960. *Photo Ken Young.*

Today No. 50 Vicarage Road is a restaurant - Goldies - on both ground and first floors. Over the years this building has had several uses. From c. 1910 to 1966, and maybe earlier, a boot and shoe maker and repairer used the ground floor. A trade directory of 1856 lists Richard Rickard as a shoemaker in Vicarage Road and in 1889 John Gill's name appears. From c. 1910 to c. 1926 William Wills was the cobbler and he was followed by William Butcher who remained there until 1966. He advertised in the church magazine of 1932 as a practical hand-sewn boot and shoe repairer.

The shop became a popular meeting place for elderly, retired people. Although most of them were members of the Miners and Mechanics Institute across the road they appreciated the

above A view through the door of the Mushroom Tea Room c. 1958.

left Elderly men stand outside the cobbler's c. 1960. l-r - Arthur Roberts, Mr Butcher the cobbler, Student Roberts, Art. Dyer, Will 'Pia' James and Fred James.

left The Cobbler's Kitchen café in 1968.

cosy atmosphere of the repair shop. The floor was like a cobbled street paved with discarded soles of boots and shoes. On his retirement in 1966 the West Briton newspaper carried a long article entitled, *"A century of shoe repairs is ended"*. It said, *"Village cobblers and village blacksmiths are becoming fewer each year and on Saturday the St Agnes cobbler shut up his little shop in Vicarage Road for the last time. Mr W C Butcher's retirement means that after more than a century the sound of leather cutting and nails being hammered into shoes will probably never be heard there again...... Not so long ago St Agnes had three boot and shoe repairing businesses. The closure of the last marks the end of an era. From beyond living memory there has been a cobbler's shop in Vicarage Road. It is part of one of the oldest buildings in St Agnes...the future of the cobbler's shop is at present not known. It would make an ideal club for elderly men if it could be secured and funds made available."*

During the time when the ground floor was a cobbler's the first floor was a barber's shop, a Bethel Gospel Chapel, a tea-room (the Mushroom Tea Room run by Clare Guard) and a boutique.

After its closure as a cobbler's shop the whole building became a café aptly named The Cobblers Kitchen. The ground floor was a kitchen, bar and small dining area and the first floor the main dining area. In 1972 the building was taken over by Miller and Co. estate agents.

Jubilee House

This house was so named because it was built in Queen Victoria's Jubilee year - 1887. There was a shop to the left of the front door but this has since been converted into a room with a bay window. (This should not be confused with the similar shop window installed next door at No. 19 in 1985) The shop sold oil, lamps, wallpaper and all kinds of decorating materials and was run by John Reynolds and his son Fred who lived next door at No. 19. They also undertook painting and decorating work. John was a very good engraver and another of his sidelines was engraving brass coffin breastplates in beautiful copperplate writing for the local undertakers.

When he was a boy Alf Bunt used to watch John doing his engraving work, he recalled, *"You weren't allowed to speak, you could breathe but that was all"*.

above Taken around 1935 this view of Vicarage Road is at its junction with British Road. A three-wheeled car has stopped outside Jubilee House and a boy looks at it with interest. A few changes to note in this picture; the iron railings outside most houses, the original entrance porch to the Meadery building, the double fronted house where Barclays Bank is today and on the extreme right, the wall of Mr Reynolds' paint store.

When eventually Fred took over the business he closed the shop and used a building on the opposite side of the road, at the top of British Road, as a store.

Later, Mr Rich from Redruth used part of the store as a fruit and greengrocery shop; he called it The Bouquet.

top Jubilee House
c. 1890. Note No. 19
next door has not yet
been built to the left.

above Reynolds' window
blinds showing the vast
array of goods and
services available.

The Oddfellows Hall

The foundation stone for the Oddfellows Hall was laid in 1881. The West Briton Newspaper of the 29th June 1881 had the following report, *"The memorial stones of a new St Agnes lodge were laid on Friday last. The site, which is in Vicarage Road, was purchased from Mr Enys, for a very moderate sum, and Bro. Richard King was entrusted with the preparation of the plans. The building will be of ordinary plain kind, 60 feet by 30 feet and is to be built from Body's stone, with Carn Marth granite dressings. The hall will seat comfortably 300 and* *there will be a pleasant approach to the building".* Within a short while the Hall was opened and used by the Loyal St Agnes Lodge of the Independent Order of Oddfellows No. 3611 - a Friendly Society. These societies have been around for hundreds of years and grew up on a simple premise that a group of people contributed to a mutual fund and then received benefits at a time of need. The early meetings were often held as social gatherings when subscriptions were paid. The Societies were

founded in villages and towns and preceded the creation of the Welfare State; they were often the only way a working person would receive help in times of ill health or old age.

The sash was the most significant item of uniform adopted by the society and was worn with pride on public and ceremonial occasions to celebrate unity, demonstrate affiliation and indicate position and status. Aprons, neck ribbons and badges were also worn. The parallels with freemasonry were deliberate, in fact by the end of the 19th century it was the Masonic warehouses that controlled the supply of these items.

The society at St Agnes formed in 1845 and continued well into the 20th century but on the 9th August 1933 the R C G Newspaper carried the following report, "*The St Agnes Oddfellows Hall has been let for the purpose of a cinema, a lodge meeting on Friday afternoon confirming the recommendation of the management committee. The adaptation of the premises is to be taken in hand at once*". The Oddfellows continued to use a room built on the back to pay their dues and for their meetings. This room was also used by Mr Harry Warren as a barbers for about six years until 1978.

above Juvenile and adult members of the Oddfellows society in Churchtown in 1910. Note the sashes and aprons worn by the adults and children. The author's great grandfather is present as a member of the society, a tall man with a bowler hat and moustache on the left of the picture, in front of the right hand window. He was also the village policeman.

The Regal Cinema & Puppet Theatre

For most of its life, until its eventual closure, Mr and Mrs Philip Taylor ran the cinema. In August 1970 Mr Taylor was interviewed by Franklin Engelmann for the BBC radio programme Down Your Way. He described the early days of the cinema. *"I have been here since 1937, it was a cinema then but originally it was an Oddfellows hall built in 1881. I didn't do the conversion from the Oddfellows hall, in fact it was running as a cinema in 1937 and started life as a cinema in the early 1930's for about three years but they didn't make a go of it and it stayed closed until 1937. Somebody else had the idea of re-opening it. We were already in the village running film shows weekly in the village hall and this opening was a great threat to us but it was the year we were going to have a successful carnival and we decided to film the carnival in colour, on 16mm film. We showed it at the Church Hall in our weekly show and packed the place, the cinema was running to nobody and as a result we had a meeting with the gentleman running it, came to an arrangement and took over their cinema and we have been running it ever since."*

Many will remember the cinema's black cat which was often seen walking across the screen during a film performance.

The cinema survived until 1978 when, on the 16th August, the building was opened to the public as "The Little Puppet Theatre". In an early programme it says, *"The newly opened Little Puppet Theatre at St Agnes offers a uniquely different outing for the whole family. Adults will find that a puppet show can be a refreshing change from conventional theatre and the cinema, while children will be enthralled by the little dramas and fantasies acted out before their eyes on a purpose built miniature stage"*.

On Tuesday the 24th April 1979 H.R.H. Prince Charles, Duke of Cornwall, paid a visit to the theatre, he spent forty minutes there during which time he tried manipulating the puppets. In 1985 the building became the Meadery owned by the Cornish Mead Company.

above The Meadery 2006.

left H R H Prince Charles, Duke of Cornwall, leaves the Little Puppet Theatre after a short visit in April 1979.
Photo Tom Thompson

Fore Street

This view shows the village being prepared for the Coronation Day celebrations in 1911. Every town and village made a whole-hearted attempt to celebrate the event. Here, flags are flying and the man on the ladder, on the left, is putting a fresh coat of paint on the building.

On the 22nd June a procession paraded the village - it was assembled in the following order: Gentlemen on horse back, Coastguards, Boys Brigade, St Agnes Band, St Agnes and Mithian Schools, members of the Friendly Societies and the general public and carriages. Everyone wanted their property to be neat and tidy as the procession went past. The property being painted by the man on the ladder, No. 23, was at one time the first Post Office in St Agnes, it was located there from the 1850s to the 1890s. It later became a butcher's, a barber's, and a newsagent/sweet shop. It ceased being a shop c. 1946 and became residential.

left c. 1930, Mrs Whitta stands in the doorway of No. 23 - she ran it as a newsagent/sweet shop with her daughter Violet. In a 1925 Church magazine she advertises as a "*Newsagent, stationer, confectioner, tobacconist and fancy dealer and will deliver all daily and weekly papers free of charge. Also, a good range of crest china.*"

FORE STREET SU

left Fore Street c. 1920.

Delbridge's Shop & Garage

From c. 1894 and for almost a hundred years, a shop at No. 41 Vicarage Road was owned by the Delbridge family. In 1977 Tom Thompson the then recorder of St Agnes Old Cornwall Society interviewed Miss E.A. Delbridge, age 79, he recorded the following information, "*Miss Delbridge's father's uncle, or grandfather, had a room in the Market House at Churchtown for shoe making and repairing. It would appear that after the Market House was demolished c. 1894, the business moved directly to No.41 Vicarage Road. When the property was bought by Mr Delbridge it was two shops, one a hatter and the other a jeweller. He then made it into one shop with two halves, one side selling ironmongery and the other selling shoes. The right hand shop originally had a small window and a door but when it was converted to the ironmongery side of the new shop these were removed and a new full width window inserted. This "new" window came from Smiths of Redruth when they were doing some alterations. Mr Deldridge didn't make shoes at the shop; he bought them from Smiths of Redruth and also sent them there for repairs. . Mr Smith had come to Redruth from Lancashire and set up a factory making clogs. Men's Hob-nailed boots sold for 5/11d a pair. Tallow candles were sold from the ironmongers together with leather sheets and rivets for D.I.Y. shoe repairs.*

Miss Delbridge sold wooden clogs; ladies' were felt lined with buckles: mens' were laced. The clogs had iron on the bottom but only around the edges and on the heels. Mr Delbridge also used to sell cakes from the side window of the shoe shop. He had the bakery business in Churchtown where he employed a baker, until the premises were destroyed by fire. He was also a shipping agent. The shop was under the charge of Miss Delbridge's father and sister; then her father and herself and the just her. In 1969 she sold the business to Peggy Thomas but stayed on for nine months to help her.

Mr Delbridge was always mechanically minded and, while at private school, would often call in at the blacksmiths and get his white starched clothes filthy. His mother thought she would "make or break" this interest by sending him to work at a blacksmith, where he shoed horses.

above Central Garage. No 42 from c.1909 to c.1924 had been a sweet shop run by Mary Stribley she also sold glass and china. Sometime around 1924 Thomas turned it into his garage and called it

Central Garage. After its closure, c. 1949, it became The Coach House Café followed by The Cornwall Café - its current name- now run by Billy Roberts.

About 60 years ago he bought the then sweet shop next to the ironmongers, No.42, and knocked the shop through into the room behind and made a garage just big enough for one car. From here he sold Shell petrol and Castrol oil. There were two petrol pumps at the front, one at each end of the original shop.

left By c.1910 when this photo was taken the large right hand window has been installed replacing the small window and door. The small shop to the right, No. 42, was later converted into a garage by Mr Delbridge.

below left Peggy Thomas has a fine display of shoes in her shop in 1985 - Cornwall Café is to the right.

top left Taken c. 1902, this view shows Mr Delbridge's shop after he had made it into one with two parts, his shoe shop on the left and the iron-mongery on the right. The ironmongery still has the original small window with a door to the right, the window from Smiths of Redruth still to be fitted.

These tanks are still there covered by steel plates. He also converted the garden at the back into a garage yard. The garden used to have a summer house and fruit trees but these were dispensed with and the garages erected one with a pit. Here he employed two men repairing cars. He also hired out cars and he enjoyed this as he was able to get out into the countryside, himself driving. The cars he owned, all bought second hand from London, included Darracq, Morris Oxford, Star(which he liked the best) and a London taxi. The garage business came to an end after the Second World War due to the shortage of fuel. The house and garage had a piped gas supply which came from their own gas-making machine in the yard at the rear. This worked due to the reaction of water on carbide. There were two concentric drums with water and carbide and it was important not to let the water level get too low or else the reaction faltered and the lamps flickered".

In 1969 Peggy Thomas took over the shoe shop. She was followed by T J Shoes until its closure as a shop in the 1990s. It is now a part of the dwelling house.

39 & 40 Vicarage Road

left Sylvia Dibbs outside her grocery shop at No. 40 c. 1935.

left Taken c. 1910 this view shows a nice sunny day in Vicarage Road. On the right is No. 40, a grocery shop owned by Richard Herbert Trenerry. The property has changed hands many times over the years but it remained basically a grocery and newsagent's shop until 1971 when, for a couple of years, it became a launderette and electrical goods shop. By 1973 it was a restaurant and has remained so ever since. Today it is called Sally's.

left A 1970 view showing the telephone kiosk outside No. 40 - before it was moved to its present site in Trelawney Road. Next door, at No. 39, is the Hi Diddle Griddle restaurant. There was also a coffee bar in the basement used by the youngsters of the village.

27 Vicarage Road

This view of No. 27 Vicarage Road, c. 1920, is of the building when it was one property, owned by John Angwin. His residence was on the right and to the left was his shop - a stationers, bookbinders and printers. In 1980 Tom Thompson, interviewed 81-year old Doris Ward, John Angwin's daughter. His notes state, *"The left hand side was built as a shop in about 1893/4, from where stationery and postcards were sold. The printing machines were over the shop except for the poster press, which was too heavy, and was in a room at the rear. The sort of items printed were bills, letter headings and posters. The Angwins decided to extend the premises by building a house adjoining the shop. In 1904 the right hand part of the property was built and the family moved there in January 1905. The site was leased from the Enys Estate and before the extension could be built, mine waste had to be removed at 6d a load. On the end of the house is a window actually fitted in a doorway, with stone in-fill below. Mr Angwin had planned to build a conservatory on the end of the house using this proposed doorway as access. However when Mrs Angwin moved into the house and realised how large it was, she said that she didn't want any extra housework and the conservatory was never built. When the separate building at the rear was built the business moved into this and the shop was turned into living accommodation, making one large house."*

The two printers who succeeded him and who used the printing works behind the house, were Arthur Evans and Josiah Sidney Repper, both of

whom had served their apprenticeship with him. About 1937 Josiah Sidney Repper moved his printing works from here to new premises opposite the post office.

top In 1987, before the building of the new pottery, the old printing works building was visible from the road.

above A view along Vicarage Road c. 1910 with the shop on the right.

The Growth of the Village

above c. 1900 - Nos. 35 to 39 Vicarage Road. Number 37 is Beacon View which, before the building of the houses on the opposite side of the road, had a clear view to the Beacon. The houses on the Beacon View side of the road appear on the 1841 Tithe Map so were obviously built before this date - some 50 years before the other side was developed.

In 1970 J E Tredinnick gave a talk to members of the Miners and Mechanics Institute about the history of St Agnes from 1820 to 1840. Although Mr Tredinnick assembled the information it was written by Isaac Rowse (1822 - 1908) with additions by John Ernest Tremewan (1876 - 1910). A copy of this talk is held in St Agnes Museum; a short extract states, "*From the post office to the old burial ground there were no houses and on the opposite side, from the post office as far as Trelawney Road, it was mine dumps and fields with the exception of the three cottages near the Oddfellows Hall or present cinema. On the site of Miss Delbridge's shop, there was a horse whim used for hoisting dirt and a few yards away there was a footway with a ladder protruding three or four feet above the surface leading to Thomas' Mine shaft. Vicarage (Road) was so called on account of it being the home of the vicar who lived in a house on the site of Dales Garage.*"

You will see by this that with the exception of two or three cottages, fields and mine dumps at one time divided the village. The area called Vicarage was at one end, in the area of the chemist today, with Churchtown at the other.

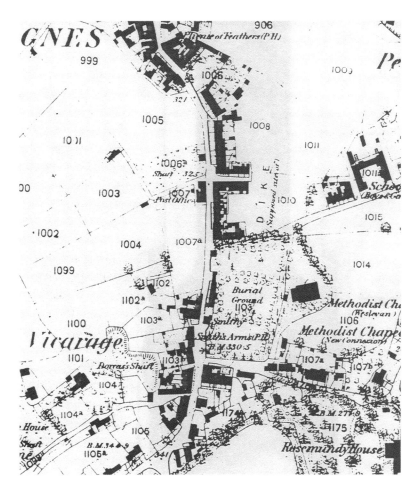

left By 1880, when this Ordnance Survey map was printed, development had taken place to the east of the road but on the opposite side, as Mr Tredinnick stated, there were just three cottages, one of which is shown as the old post office.

below c. 1905 - Nos. 32 to 34 Vicarage Road. Number 34, on the right, has been the home of the Whitworth family and the Doctor's residence for over a hundred and twenty years.

The Shops Opposite the Post Office

Flags are flying in this 1911 view towards the post office with preparation still ongoing for the Coronation celebrations. A ladder rests against the end wall of the thatched cottage and the newly whitewashed wall is almost finished with just the chimney to complete in readiness for the big day.

This cottage was one of five that stood where the toilets are now located, they stretched down the road to join the house now called Chegwyn. From c. 1900 to 1909 James Tredinnick had it as a butcher's shop but in February 1909 the row of cottages caught fire. The Royal Cornwall Gazette newspaper of the 25th February included the following account, "*St Agnes was saved from a fire on Monday, which if it had not been so promptly extinguished, would probably have threatened the destruction of a considerable part of Churchtown. A steam roller was engaged in scarifying the bit of rising ground between Churchtown and the Church Schoolroom when a spark from the engine is said to have fallen on one of the thatched houses, which are close to the road and occupied by Mr Henry Letcher - Jeweller, Mr Tredinnick - butcher, and Mr Penhaligan and others. The thatch being dry was ablaze in minutes. Mr Penhaligan immediately got on the roof*

and began tearing away at the burning thatch, a work in which he was ably assisted by Mr C Chegwyn. Water was drawn off the standpipe and passed hand to hand and thrown on the fire which was in this way soon extinguished. The furniture in the house occupied by Mr Penhaligan was damaged by water thrown on the roof."

Fortunately the building was saved but it needed a few repairs. The following month, on the 18th March, the R C G newspaper reported that, "*Fred James had purchased the butchery from James Tredinnick*". You will remember that just four months earlier, in October 1908, Fred James had also had a disastrous fire, at his butcher's shop at the other end of the village; the thought of another thatched roof and possible fire obviously didn't worry him. It remained a butcher's until the 1930s when it became a fish and chip shop and another fire broke out. After this disaster the owner, Mr Wilcox, moved his business to the shop at the end of the bakery.

Around 1936/37 all five cottages were demolished, the top two becoming the site of the public toilets.

CHURCH TOWN ST. AGNES.

above The front of the butcher's shop that once stood opposite the post office c. 1910.

left View to the post office in 2006.

The Cottages Opposite the Post Office

A very rare view of the row of cottages that once stood opposite the post office. The only one remaining is the dark building on the right called Chegwyn - situated near Costcutters store. After these three cottages were demolished c. 1936 the site was bought by Mrs Jessie Repper. A new shop and printing works was built for her son, Sidney, and he moved there from the site he rented from John Angwin. In 1985 Mrs Repper's grandson wrote to the author with the following information, *"Between 1936 and 1937 my grandmother had the house and the shop built by Mr J E Tredinnick who was a local builder and lived around the Beacon. The printing works, which was situated behind the shop, was built by one of Jessie Repper's sons, Mr Rubin Repper, who lives at Truro. He built this for his twin brother, Sidney, who served his apprenticeship with John Angwin. I can remember the move of the printing equipment from Angwin's to the new printing works, I was about eight at the time and there was a good many men, lifting gear and all sorts of equipment to move the heavy equipment a couple hundred yards down the road. In those days there were no traffic problems so the move was not too difficult."*

right An advertisement for the shop in a 1950s St Agnes guide.

FOR—

Printing	Tobacco
Stationery	Cigarettes
Toys	Views. etc.

J. S. REPPER

Printer and Stationer
CHURCHTOWN. ST. AGNES

Phone 339

below Jessie Repper and
her daughter outside their
new shop in 1937 - seen
here decorated for the
Coronation.

below For many years
nothing was built on the
piece of ground next to
the shop, in front of the
printing works. Today
Malcolm and Ginette
hairdressers occupy the
site.

below right The row in
2006.

right The printing works
at the rear of the shop
c. 1937. It ceased being a
print works c. 1963 and
since then has been used
by several types of
businesses. From 1991 to
2006 it was Elegance
Health and Beauty Salon
run by Jan and Suzannah
Ball.

The Post Office

In 1844 there was a Receiver of Mail but in an 1856 Trade Directory Thomas Angwin is recorded as postmaster and grocer in Vicarage. In 1873 the Directory of Cornwall shows that Thomas Stribley had taken over both these roles. During this period letters went to the Scorrier Station Sorting Office before being brought daily to St Agnes by pony or donkey and cart.
It would seem that the first post office was in Vicarage or Vicarage Road, next to what is now the Meadery. It certainly appears here on the 1880 Ordnance Survey map.

In the 1890s it moved to a shop in Churchtown, where the greengrocery shop is today - opposite Costcutters. It remained there until 1903 when it moved to its present site.

The post office not only dealt with the written message, it was also involved in the spoken word with the opening of the first telephone exchange in 1928. At first there were twenty-three subscribers:

1   The Post Office
2   Dales Garage Vicarage Road
3
4   Doctor Cuthbert Whitworth
5   J T Letcher & Sons - Grocer Peterville
6   St Agnes Hotel
7   Cowl - Baker Churchtown
8   Reynolds - Grocer Vicarage Road
10   Railway Hotel Vicarage Road
11   Kemps - Grocer and Tea Rooms Quay
12
13   The Police House
14   E W Friston - Builders Merchant Polberro
15   W H Newton - Garage Peterville
16
17   Cornwall County Council Maternity Home Rosemundy
18   J E Tredinnick - Builder Sunholme Goonvrea
19
20   St Agnes Coastguard Station
21   T J Delbridge - Central Garage Vicarage Road
22
23   Charles James - Carrier & Car Hire Vicarage Road

In many cases people didn't know the number of the person they wanted, they just knew that they were on the phone and would ask the operator for them by name - i.e. Dales Garage or St Agnes Hotel etc.

top The post office at Churchtown c. 1902.

above The post office at its present location c. 1910. Note the steps from the door leading down to the road.

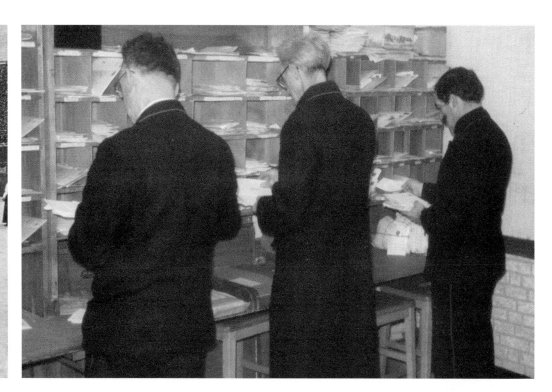

above Reg Roberts talking to the postman outside the post office in the 1950s. Reg was married to the Sub-Postmistress Dorothy Roberts (nee Stribley).

top Ron Luke, Charlie Bunt and John Redfern sort the mail in the 1960s. *Photo Bill Morrison*

Below the Post Office

above A lorry gets stuck outside Westwoods in the mid 1970's. Fortunately Claude Tonkin was working locally with his Michigan and clears the obstruction by lifting the rear of the lorry around.

above left Prout sweet shop c. 1900. Other photos show this as Prout and Rogers - situated below the post office. By 1912 Miss Sarah Rowe ran it; she sold Tom Trot, sweets, cordials and jams. It is now a part of a dwelling.

far left The mail cart and milk cart outside the post office c. 1905. John Angwin stands on the far right and his daughter, Doris Angwin (Mrs Ward), is in the foreground on the right.

left c. 1910 the milk delivery wagon stands outside no. 23 Churchtown, a sweet shop owned by Miss Sarah Rowe.

Westwoods

For at least 130 years No. 4 Churchtown has been a grocer's and general store; the front of the building remained unchanged for many years. This picture, taken in the late 1930s, shows Daniel and Ethel McAlister in the doorway of the shop; they were there from 1934 to 1941. The telephone number 23 is above the door; this must have been taken over when Charles James ceased his carrier and car hire business.

In 1942 Harold Westwood moved there and by 1952 he had it modernised to its present form. Tommy Coombe acquired it in 1958.

In the top right picture, taken c. 1958, to the left of the shop is a two-storey building - No. 3. For over one hundred and fifty years it had been used by a tailor, greengrocer and fruiterer and a grocer and from 1926 to 1958 it was a drapery and haberdashery shop run by the Misses Hilda

and Ethel James. These two ladies became a legend in their own lifetime. One story told of how they would lower a basket out of the upstairs window in which would be placed the tradesmen's wares, the money for payment would then be lowered in a tin can on a piece of string. They also made friends with and tamed the rats that ran around the house.

By 1958 the building was empty and derelict and when Mr Coombe bought the shop, Westwoods, he purchased this building as well. In 1960 he had it demolished as it had become unsafe and there was a risk of children lighting fires there. He then built a garage and store room on the site.

top Westwood's store
c.1958

above Mike and Ann Bunt
outside Costcutters in
2006. They ran the shop
from 1996 to 2006.

Women's Institute Square

The building comprising the Women's Institute on the first floor and the shop on the ground floor is of considerable age and was registered as a Building of Architectural and Historic Interest in 1968.

At the beginning of the last century the ground floor was a butcher's shop but by 1947 it was a hairdresser's, used initially by Archibald Williams and then by Henry Prisk - in the late 1950s and 1960s. The author well remembers the day when he was tall enough not to have to use the plank of wood placed across the arms of the chair but could sit on the padded seat so that Henry could cut his hair.

After 1970 it became a hobby shop, hardware shop, greengrocer and fruiterer and today it is a jeweller's shop called Little Feathers
From the early 1900s until 1928 the first floor was a corn and grocery store for the shop across the road - now Costcutters. For a few years before and during the First World War it was the Liberal Association reading room.

Alf Bunt remembered the building, "*It was owned by Timo Thomas and the Women's Institute, as it is now; it used to be the stores for the shop. They used to drive over in their pony and wagon and under the bridgeway and pull the stuff up through the floor.*"

In a talk to St Agnes Women's Institute in 1951 Matt Radcliffe recalled, "*The Woman's Institute building belonged to a political club and later it was a corn store. The space in front was known as Market Strand and booths were set up there, and there was a cheap jack, on pay day.*" The author has also seen the area referred to as Market Square.

The Women's Institute album of 1951 states, "*The Institute was formed on 17th January 1924 by Miss Whitburn with a membership of twenty five, Mrs Whitworth being the first of a line of Presidents that served it well...At first members met in various private houses but the acquisition of premises in 1928 gave the movement increased facilities and it has made steady progress... The monthly meetings are very well attended, the talks cover a wide field and the social half hour and competitions give scope for talent and ingenuity.*"

bottom David Rees in the doorway of his Hardware and D I Y shop c. 1980. *Photo Bill Morrison.*

left Numbers 20 and 21 in Churchtown Square c. 1926. For many years until c. 1891 No 20, on the left, was the Plume of Feathers, one of many public houses in Churchtown.

When this photo was taken c. 1926 it was a boarding house and tearoom run by George Green. The shop on the right, No. 21, is Edmond Mark Uglow's gentleman's outfitters. Previously his shop was in what is now the bar of the St Agnes Hotel. He left the shop c. 1934 to build a new one in Vicarage Road. Prior to his use it had been a grocery shop, a boot and shoe repairers, the post office and a druggist.

Churchtown Market

From time immemorial a weekly street market was held at St Agnes on a Thursday. The market standings, as the stalls were called, stretched along Churchtown, from what is now Costcutters to the St Agnes Hotel, on both sides of the road and around the Square. Market standings came as a right with the property in Churchtown, when a building came up for sale they were included.

The following advertisement appeared in the R C G Newspaper in April 1834 under the heading, *"Desirable property in St Agnes"*. It said, *"Lot 2, all that stone-built dwelling house now occupied by Mrs Ann Roberts, together with three shops adjoining. The above premises are situated in St Agnes, Churchtown,* and have the right to fixed stalls on the market ground in front."

The historian Thomas Tonkin of Trevaunance said of Churchtown, *"There has been time out of mind, in this little town which consists of about forty houses, a weekly market kept for all sorts of wares, and victuals, except corn, on Thursdays, which induced me in 1706 to endeavour to get a Patent for a market on the said day and two fairs yearly"*. The Queen duly signed it but a petition from Truro stopped it. Thomas Tonkin added, *"...underhand opposed by the very same person who had promised me their assistance in it; and so it has rested ever since to the no small loss of the whole parish"*. Nonetheless, ordinary weekly markets continued.

above The Market House entrance c. 1880.

Market day on a Thursday didn't suit everyone - unfortunately St Agnes miners were paid on a Friday or Saturday. In 1830 two mine captains decided to organise a Saturday market for the benefit of the locals, it proved to be a great success as this letter to the Editor of the R C G Newspaper on the 30th October shows.

"Dear Sir, Perhaps it might be gratifying to the inhabitants of this and neighbouring parishes to learn that this market we announced, took place on Saturday last, and that, not withstanding the shortness of the notice and the advertisement having appeared in the journals only the same or previous days, it was attended by many respectable vendors and a great number of purchasers, thereby evinced their approval of the arrangements.

At so short a notice it may be inferred the greater number of vendors who attended on Thursday could not make arrangements for filling their stands; the same may be applied to purchasers; but as proof of support which the public will afford to the Saturday market, it will be sufficient to observe that the whole of the goods offered on the first trial was readily sold.

Much credit is due to the mine captain, who together with his coadjunctors, have in contemplation the building of a market house on an extensive scale, for the convenience of both buyer and seller."

Within a very short time a market house of considerable size had been built on a piece of wasteland in front of the Church. It wasn't the best site; it stood in front of the Church, almost hiding it. The 1841 census states that a Mr Tonkin was employed as the caretaker of the Market House; he also lived in the building.

It is not known how long the Saturday markets were held but those on a Thursday appear to have continued right up to the end of the 19th century.

Mrs Moore, reminiscing for the Woman's Institute book of 1951, described the Thursday market held in the Market House, *"The village was crowded. Fruit and vegetables and meat were sold and later, when the market house was taken down, meat was still sold from a wooden booth in front of the hotel."*

In 1894 the Market House was purchased by the Vicar and Churchwardens for £250 and, with the help of a gift of £100 from Sir Edwin Durning-Lawrence, it was demolished. This then made way for road widening and a better access to the Church.

Churchtown Over the Years

The next few pages include a selection of photographs taken from roughly the same location in Churchtown and showing the changes that have taken place over the years.

above c. 1880 showing the end of the Market House opposite the Commercial Hotel. Note the stall on the right and what appears to be a stone built, slate roofed market standing in the Square.

top Another early view c. 1890; by this time John Paull is the licensee of the Hotel and his name appears above the entrance.

above By c. 1906 the Market House had been demolished, the road widened and a new Church wall with railings built. In this view you can clearly see the road with cobbles or paving on either side. Until 1852 the whole of Churchtown was paved however in January of that year the Board of Highways resolved that, *"The pitch paving in the Churchtown be taken up and instead of pitch paving the street be macadamised and a neat curb of stones be laid on each side".* Here three girls stand in the middle of the road and pose for the photographer - Mr Sammy Solway.

Churchtown Over the Years

above By 1930 John Paull has long since ceased to be the licensee of the hotel but it still bears his name; it changed to the St Agnes Hotel not long after this picture was taken. By now the shop has gone from the left of the hotel and the area it occupied made a part of the bar. The building on the right of the view, the paper shop today, is a dwelling with a front door and window.

CHURCHTOWN, ST. AGNES.

above By the late 1940s Mr Westwood owns the shop on the left. Cobbles and stone still form the pavement of the shop next door.

left The posters on the wall tell us that this photo was taken in late August 1954. Nicky Thomas' shop now has a proper pavement outside.

below Churchtown in 2006.

Churchtown Stores

above This photograph taken c. 1914 shows that No. 5 has changed very little over the years. It is interesting to note that there is a concrete pavement outside the shops at either end of the row of shops but not outside No 5 - it would be a further forty years before they got theirs.

Churchtown Arts today is housed in No. 5 Churchtown, one of the village's oldest and interesting buildings. One of its rooms had eighteenth century newspapers pasted on the wall under the wallpaper and there is also a small portion of barrel-vaulted ceiling in the back of the shop. When the roof was re - tiled a pair of children's button-up boots were found (it was an old custom to place a pair of boots in the roof for good luck and prosperity) and these were replaced after the work was finished. The exterior has changed very little over the years. In 1997 during its conversion into the art and craft centre a secret room and other interesting features were discovered. The West Briton of the

above Miss Edith Pope, later Mrs Shrimpton, stands in Churchtown Square in July 1924. The shop behind her at this time was a grocery, drapery and general household merchant's owned by Matthew Pope Radcliffe. He had run the shop from 1912 to 1937 when it was taken over by Nicholas (Nicky) Thomas.

12th June 1997 under the heading, *"Secret room found as ancient building is converted"* carried the following report, *"Records for Churchtown Stores in St Agnes, which has reopened displaying the work of local artists, go back to the 1400's. A secret upper room was discovered during the restoration, which was overseen by the owner Jill Treleaven. It had been totally blocked up. There was no door or lintel, just the outline of a bricked - in window. No skeleton was found, but staff are puzzled as to the room's purpose. A former blacksmith's shop in one corner of the renovated ground floor has now been fully uncovered. It has an intact original slate floor and one of only two barrel ceilings in the county - shaped to help funnel out the smoke. The oldest part is in the rear courtyard. Shoppers have been peering at the courtyard buildings once used as houses. One woman had lived in one as a child".*

above, left Nicky Thomas in his shop at Churchtown in the late 1960s. In 1971 he sold the business to Charlie Bunt.

above Churchtown Stores in 1985. As far back as 1856 this shop was a grocer, draper and general household merchant and remained so until its change to Churchtown Arts.

You will notice that part of the metal frame of the very old window, on the right, is pushed in. Alf Bunt said in 1983 that this was done by a bullock, *"They used to drive bullocks down behind the butcher's shop and put 'em quiet' (slaughter them) and* then sell them in the shop. They tell me years ago that a bullock was up there and he didn't want to go down the yard and he turned around and pushed his rump against the shop window and pushed that window back like that. I don't think they've straightened it now, it was never straightened in Nicky Thomas' time anyhow." The window is the same today.

Butcher & Paper Shop Churchtown

above The Band of Hope march through Churchtown in 1912 on route to their tea. Everyone is in their best Sunday clothes and wearing some form of headgear. Behind the parade on the left is a shop. This has been a butcher's shop for over a hundred years and to the right was the living accommodation with a grand front door and a window to the side. When Alwyn Harris became the butcher there in the 1930s he knocked out the small window, put in a new front and made a shop for his mother-in-law, Mrs Whitta. She then moved here from her shop next to the Oddfellows Hall.

left c. 1950 Ben Sargeant has a fine display of meat and poultry hanging in his window.

left This postcard dated 1959 shows the newsagent, confectioner and tobacconist when Mr Johns ran it. The card was sent to Dorset with the following message, "*We have been to Newquay and Perranporth, Newquay is terribly crowded just like Margate. Still we are having a good cup of tea here and the views are lovely, wish I could paint.*" Things don't change.

far left Mrs Whitta outside her shop in Churchtown.

The White Hart Hotel

This was once the most famous hotel and public house in St Agnes.

In October 1778 an advertisement appeared in the Sherborne Mercury Newspaper. *"To be let for a term of 7, 14, or 21 years from Christmas next all that well accustomed Inn with good stables, brew house and a convenient back yard called The White Hart in St Agnes Churchtown, now in possession of Mr William Argall, who is about to quit the same next Christmas."*

At this time it would have been a much smaller building than it is today and probably thatched but, as you will see by this advertisement, it had stables and a brew house. Shortly after, c. 1789, it was rebuilt to its present form. These alterations were carried out at least thirty years before those of its neighbour, the Kings Arms (St Agnes Hotel), and it became the most modern hotel in the village and consequently attracted most of the auctions and functions that were held in St Agnes at the time. In The Journal of St Agnes Museum Trust No. 4, Frank Carpenter has written a detailed history of the hotel. He says, *"During the early years of the nineteenth century the local monthly magistrate's court was held at the White Hart. It was here those charged with minor offences i.e. drunkenness, causing a nuisance, etc. came before the law - the Parson and Squire Peter who were two of those who sat on the bench. If found guilty the miscreant was taken outside and placed in the stocks which were sited in front of the Church opposite the White Hart. This practice was discontinued in the 1830s. This of course was before the Church was rebuilt or the Market House erected in front of the Church."*

During the 1800s and early 1900s there was a succession of landlords but none stayed more than a few years.

Frank Carpenter continued, *"It was in 1923 that the death knell of the White Hart as a public house was first sounded, when Mr Edward C Edyvean became landlord of Paull's Hotel and at the same time his wife became licensee of the White Hart. The first record of the Inn becoming a Private Hotel was in the 1925 St Agnes Official Guide where it is described as the White House Private Hotel. Since this time it has become known as the Porthvean Hotel."*

above When this photo of the White Hart Hotel was taken c. 1905 William Butland was the licensee and his name is over the door. Barrels are being unloaded from the horse and wagon outside and a child sits on a second slewed across the road

top The White Hart Hotel on the left c. 1920. You will notice that there is a fairly steep slope from the road level and just two steps to the front door. At some point this slope has been taken down level with the road and a patio area created with a flight of four stairs up to it.

above By the time this postcard was produced in the early 1930s the hotel was called the Porthvean Private Hotel. All major alterations to this hotel and the St Agnes Hotel next door have been completed and this view has changed very little over the last seventy years.

Paull's Hotel

above A 1905 postcard taken by photographer Mr Bragg of Illogan. In the centre of the view is Paull's Hotel, now the St Agnes Hotel, an Inn for at least 200 years. At one time it was called the Kings Arms and was rebuilt about 1825 when the thatched roof was replaced with slate.

c. 1844 it became Pearce's Hotel, after the landlord John Pearce, then the Commercial Hotel, then Paull's Hotel, after the landlord John Paull, and finally, in 1930, the St Agnes Hotel.

top, middle A very early 'carte de visite' photograph of the hotel. On the rear is stamped the name J Mitchell of Pydar Street, Truro. In Professor Charles Thomas' book *Views and Likenesses* about early photographers in Cornwall; it states that John Mitchell was a photographer in Pydar Street, Truro, in the 1850s and 1860s. This makes this photograph one of the earliest views in this book. Wooden scaffolding tied together with rope has been erected in front of the hotel and a man with a hammer in his hand is ready to climb the ladder.

The purpose of this scaffolding is not clear but there appears to be a platform at the top window level. Whatever is happening it has attracted a crowd either to watch the work or to have their photograph taken, an unusual occurrence at this time.

Number 9 Churchtown is to the left of the picture, it has a large shop window with small panes of glass. The building is now a dwelling house.

right A close-up of Paull's Hotel c. 1920 when the front left side was a tailor's and gentleman's outfitters run by Mark Uglow. It would appear he moved from here to No. 21 Churchtown in the early 1920s, when the area of the hotel occupied by him was converted into a bar.

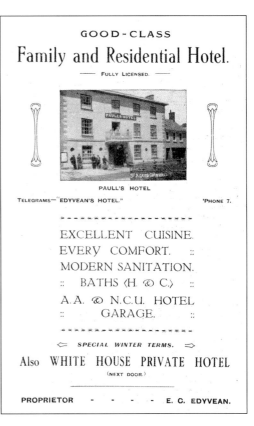

GOOD-CLASS
Family and Residential Hotel.

—— FULLY LICENSED. ——

PAULL'S HOTEL

TELEGRAMS—"EDYVEAN'S HOTEL."   'PHONE 7.

- -

EXCELLENT   CUISINE.
EVERY   COMFORT.   ::
MODERN SANITATION.
::   BATHS (H. & C.)   ::
A.A. & N.C.U. HOTEL
::   GARAGE.   ::

- -

⇐   SPECIAL WINTER TERMS.   ⇒

Also WHITE HOUSE PRIVATE HOTEL
(NEXT DOOR.)

PROPRIETOR   -   -   -   -   -   E. C. EDYVEAN.

above This advertisement appeared in the 1925 St Agnes Official Guide. The picture in the advertisement shows a small window which has replaced the shop window. Note also the special winter terms for the White House Private Hotel next door.

The Church Struck by Lightning

Very little is known about the earliest beginnings of St Agnes Church and the date of the first building is lost in antiquity. In Maurice Bizley's booklet, Portrait of a Village Church, it says, *"It must however have been before 1331 as there is an account, in Bishop Grandisson's register, of that year, of a visitation to St Agnes Church which was described as sadly neglected. From earliest times (until 1846) St Agnes, while being the chief centre of population of the large parish of Perranzabuloe, was but a chapelry of that parish, and the tutelage of the mother church was always resented."*

In 1846 St Agnes became an independent parish and the connection with Perranzabuloe was severed. At that time a 15th century church stood on the site and a faculty to demolish it was obtained. On the 4th August 1848 a building committee was appointed consisting of the Vicar, Churchwardens and eight others and within a fortnight the demolition of the old church had begun.

Writing in the St Agnes Official Guide of 1925 the Revd W H Browne said, *"The old materials were re-used and the building considerably enlarged. Fortunately these 19th century vandals left the west wall of the Nave and the Tower standing and incorporated them into the new church."* A new, finely tapering spire was built on the tower and the Lord Bishop of Exeter dedicated the church in 1851.

At about 12 midday on Wednesday the 15th March 1905 lightning struck the spire. A newspaper report of the occurrence said, *"A flash of lightning of blinding brilliancy was followed immediately by a thunderclap of tremendous force, reminding some of the noise made on the occasion of the dynamite explosion at Perranporth some years ago. The shock was so great that one person was knocked down and others were almost thrown down. The greatest damage however was done to the steeple of the Parish Church. This was struck by the electric fluid*

and about eight feet of the top of the steeple, in addition to the vane, was carried away. Nearly the whole of the debris fell upon the roof of the building. But this being strongly built, only a few comparatively small holes were made."

The following week, on the 23rd March, the R C G reported, *"A steeplejack arrived on Saturday afternoon and removed the loose stone on the top of the steeple. He found it very difficult to find a firm hold for the cramps to hold the ladders, showing that the steeple had a greater shock than those who inspected it on Friday were prepared to admit. He gave his opinion that the steeple was unsafe and that it would be dangerous to hold the normal services in the church. The Vicar, Revd Alfred Rudall, gave notice that the Church would be closed and services would be held in the schoolroom."*

The damage must have been considerable and by the 6th April the same newspaper reported, *"The taking down of the damaged steeple and part of the battlement of the tower was completed on*

Wednesday last and this part of the church now presents a very dilapidated appearance. The Steeplejack, Mr Larkins of Bow, London, has stated that the blow must have been of so tremendous a force as there was not a sound joint to be found in the bottom of the steeple. So badly was it shaken that it surprised him that the whole structure had not fallen. It made it difficult and dangerous to work with the bottom so insecure."

The steeple was eventually rebuilt and remained until 1929 when it was again struck by lightning. The top six feet fell to the ground but this time the rest of the steeple was undamaged and only the top needed to be rebuilt.

top left The Church in 1905 after being struck by lightning with the top of the steeple missing. A group of people stand by the church wall including a postmen and two miners - note the candles in their hats. The iron railings on the wall were removed during the Second World War.

middle The steeple was so badly damaged by the lightning strike in 1905 that it had to be completely demolished and rebuilt. This very unusual view shows the Church without its steeple - just the 15th century tower.

above Lightning does strike in the same place twice. In 1929 the Church was struck again but this time only the top six feet or so had to be replaced and here we see the steeplejacks at work. There was no need to scaffold the entire steeple this time - just the top section. The pinnacle weighing half a ton, which was dislodged from the top, fell through the church roof. It now stands in the corner outside the Church to the north side of the tower

Back of Town

Taken c. 1912 this view across Churchtown shows, in the centre, No 9 to the left of the present day Porthvean Hotel; it was built or rebuilt in its present form about 1798. For a time in the nineteenth century it was the Ship Inn, one of Churchtown's six public houses. For many years it was split into three, a dwelling at the rear and two shops facing Churchtown. To the right was a barber's shop run by Elisha Rickard, his barber's pole projects from the front of the building. To the left was a general store for many years, it was run by Tom Benney and then by Thomas Quick who was a greengrocer and fruiterer. By the 1920s the whole house had become residential.

To the left of this house is a lane which meanders past some lovely old whitewashed cottages at the rear of the St Agnes Hotel. In a letter to Liz Thompson in 1997 the National Trust, who now own these cottages, refer to them as being situated in Park Lane. It now serves the council houses but at that time it just led to a few cottages and fields.

In the 1925 St Agnes Guide Miss A M Bulkley writes an interesting description of this area. *"Back of the Town is the name given to a quiet corner where there is a colony of old cottages with pretty gardens and an artist's studio, which was originally a store house for silver-sand and until recently a stable. Here also is an old water tub where the cows pause on the way to and from the pastures. Looking down from this point is the most picturesque view of the town that can be had. The irregular groupings of the houses, the old roofs, the ivy clad chimneys, and the graceful spire of the Church are most attractive as seen from here and the mellow colour is very satisfying. Visitors often say it looks just like a foreign place but as their remarks are meant to be complimentary it would be better for them to say that it looked just like Cornwall and expect to find the same everywhere here. This part is reached from the main street by two sunken footpaths known as Park Lane and Church Walk. Beyond is Back Lane which passes another studio (a converted blacksmith's shop) and then only to meadows. This makes a pretty walk to Chapel Porth, by the first line of stiles, then over the shoulder of the Beacon."*

ST. AGNES.

In 1926 a pottery was opened in a building at the top of the lane. The St Agnes Women's Institute album of 1951 carried the following article, *"Miss Helen Bulkley, an artist of repute started the wayside pottery in 1926. An article in the News Chronicle of the 17th February 1939 headed, 'Beauty from Cornish Clay', stated, 'Miss Helen Bulkley turns Cornish Miners Clay into all sorts of practical and beautiful articles at the Wayside Potteries, St Agnes'. She said, 'I think I am the only*

left Tom Benney in his hat and white jacket stands outside his shop at No. 9 Churchtown c. 1905. He is reputed to have had in his shop a clock with no hands and a sign that said *"No Tick"* (no credit). Magnification of the window in this photograph reveals a sign that says, *"Please do not ask for Trust as refusal often offends"*.

left Miss Helen Bulkley outside the pottery c. 1930.

far left Miss Helen Bulkley working inside her pottery c. 1930.

person who uses Cornish Clay of this kind for fancy pottery, it is known as Miner's Clay because before the miners had safety lamps they used it to stick candles on the front of their hats. It is dug out of cliffs near here.' Miss Bulkley made many experiments with glaze. She often used Cornish minerals such as copper, iron and tin for colouring matter. For the past two years, the Wayside Potteries belonged to Mrs Homer who produces beautiful pottery for domestic use."

Helen was a sister to Annette Mabel Bulkley

who had written this article for the 1925 St Agnes Guide.

On the 29th April 1944 the Misses Bulkley gave the pottery building and the cottages where they lived in Park Lane to the National Trust.

The Road Surface at Churchtown

above New Connexion Sunday School Tea at Churchtown in 1911; the whole parade stops to have their picture taken. Note the width of the cobbled pavement and the make-up of the road itself. The boy in the centre of the view appears to be standing in a purpose-built roadside drain. W H Comer is the licensee of Paull's Hotel; he was there from c. 1908 to 1912.

top When this photo was taken in 1920 the road still hadn't been improved greatly with a rough surface and uneven stone curbs on either side. A water standpipe is positioned by the Church wall.

above By 1936 many changes had taken place. The road surface and edges had been greatly improved, the standpipe removed and a lych-gate built at the Church entrance. Erected in 1935 the wood above the entrance is inscribed,

"*In memory of George Coulter Hancock - this lych-gate was erected by his son of the same name 1935*".
Electric poles and wires are also visible; a supply was first brought to St Agnes in 1927 for Wheal Kitty Mine and at the end of 1928 for the village.

14 Churchtown

780. ST AGNES.

In this 1920s view a lady walks through Churchtown heading towards No. 14 - the shop to the left of the bakery. In the early 1900s this was the St Agnes Restaurant run by James Hooper and sons - he also had the bakery next door. Between c. 1923 and 1926 the Misses Hilda and Ethel James ran this shop as a draper's but in 1926 William Henry Cowl purchased it together with the bakery and Bakery Cottage. The two ladies then moved to No.3 Churchtown. Mr Cowl used the shop as a restaurant and tearoom and the family continued this use until about 1960. In 1967 David Gardner ran it as a photographic and gift shop and by the early 1970s Noel Rutherford had taken it over and called it Castaways; it sold arts, crafts and gifts.

On Sunday the 12th November 1972 there was a disastrous fire and in Ivan Rabey's book, *Cornwall's Fire Brigade*, it says, "*Just before 5.00 pm a passer-by saw smoke billowing from the roof of Castaways Gift Shop in the centre of St Agnes. As the nearest unit, Perranporth, as well as Truro and Camborne, were committed elsewhere, this shout was answered by the Redruth brigade. The journey was a difficult one in a gale force wind and heavy rain and the first appliances found the premises well alight; Camborne, Truro and Perranporth were soon involved and 25 firemen using three jets and two hose reels brought the blaze under control in 40 minutes although much damage was done.*"

The building was so badly damaged that it had to be completely demolished and the site was left as open ground for many years. The author has memories of a crockery smashing competition on this land during the 1977 Jubilee Celebrations. In the early 1980s a shop with accommodation above was built to a very similar design to the original. More recently the shop sold fudge, ice cream, clothes and dolls and traded under the name Indulgence.

above David Gardner's shop c. 1967.

top Firemen tackle the fire at Castaways on the 12th November 1972. *Photo Brian Cadby.*

above The badly damaged Castaways building after the fire

Bank House

above Churchtown c. 1912 showing Bank House on the left, so called because on Thursday market days it became a bank. The temporary facility operated from Mrs Grace Cowling's front room - the tenant of the house. Kelly's Directory of 1897 states that the Cornish Bank was there on Thursdays from 11.00 am - 2.00 pm; George Coulter Hancock was the agent. By 1906 the Capital and Counties Bank was offering the service there. In the 1800s the building had been yet another public house - the White Lion.

For several years until the 1940s Mr Gee used it for his dental surgery - on a Saturday between 2.00 pm and 6.00 pm.

In 1934 the owner, Mrs Downs, advertised Bank House in the St Agnes Guide, "*Near sea, beach and buses. Central for exploring the South and North coasts. Good cooking and every attention. Indoor sanitation, highly recommended, Terms Moderate*".

above A view looking down on Churchtown c. 1960. Percy James sells electrical goods in the shop that is now occupied by Estate Agents Lee and Co. In the bottom right corner is a grocer's shop run by William J Martin; he had been there since the 1930s.

There was two-way traffic through the village at this time with a finger post by the Church wall sending vehicles up the main street - heading for Truro.

top Bank House c. 1937.

The Bakery

The Bakery has been at its present location for over a hundred years. James Hooper and his sons were the bakers from c. 1906 to c. 1910 and Thomas John Delbridge followed them.

In 1917 Mr Delbridge's bakery burnt to the ground and the R C G of the 19th September included a report under the heading, *"Destruction of Bakehouse"*. It read, *"A bakehouse at St Agnes, in the occupation of Mr T J Delbridge, was burnt down on Thursday night. Mr Perry, an employee, who left the premises at about 9.30 pm, noticed no evidence of an impending outbreak of fire. At about a quarter past ten, however, Mr H Gripe observed a flickering light and called the proprietor. They found the house well alight when they returned. Two delivery vans and a motor car were got out and then water was thrown on the burning building. Mr Delbridge drove to Redruth as soon as possible and gave the alarm to the fire brigade who arrived at the scene at 1.40 am remaining until 5.00 am. In the meantime rafters of an adjoining house caught fire but after some of the slates were removed the flames were extinguished with buckets of water. Among the prominent helpers were Messrs C Chegwyn, M G Hodge, Chief Officer Ward and Police Constable Benney. A number of ladies and others helped to keep the fire under control and assisted with the carrying of water."*

Alf Bunt recalled, *"The bakery was owned by Delbridge, the one who owned the shoe shop up the*

street. I was a boy when it caught fire and she burnt to the ground. There was a standpipe over by the church, where the lychgate is now, and all we kids, if we were big enough to carry a bucket of water, we'd carry water. Well it was as well we didn't. We were carrying the buckets of water and giving them to the men to put the fire out but by the time the fire brigade got there by horse, she was down to ashes."

It is interesting to note that Mr Delbridge had to drive to Redruth to inform the Fire Brigade, no telephones yet in St Agnes. In Michael Tangye's book *Victorian Redruth* it says that at this

far left The bakery corner c. 1950. Flags fly for the carnival and three shire horses walk past. Note the double doors where the entrance to the bakery is today and where the delivery wagons would have been kept.

bottom left Moris Davis outside the bakery beside the donkey pulling the baker's barrow. Originally this was a handbarrow but shafts were added and donkey power replaced manpower much to the relief of the person who previously had to push it around the village.

left The bakery delivery wagon when Thomas Delbridge was the baker. On the side of the wagon he describes himself as a Scientific Baker.

following report under the heading, "*Wagon overturns. The accident to Mr W H Cowl is fortunately not quite as serious as was first feared. His horse ran away at Silverwell and the wagon going over the bank overturned. Mr Cowl who was driving was thrown out and being entangled in the reins was drawn for some distance on the ground.*"

In November 1971 an article appeared in the Independent newspaper under the heading, "*The Early Birds,*" it said, "*It is 5.00 am - pitch black. The only sound is of surf pounding the beach and the wind bending the trees. Only fools or maniacs would venture out at this unearthly hour, or would they? A mouth-watering smell of baked bread suddenly greets you in the freezing pre-dawn of St Agnes. It drifts from an old stone bake-house, opposite the church in this North Cornwall Village. It is a warm cheerful refuge where Mr Cecil Cowl works most mornings baking bread and saffron cakes...The little stone bakery has been run by the Cowls for many years and must be one of a few bakeries not gobbled up by combines. In the summer the place is quite a tourist attraction. Co-proprietors are Mr Stanley Cowl and Mr Moris Davis. Both are proud of the certificates won for the quality of their bread. They talk fondly of days of youth when the entire bread-making process was by hand. Today the machine is moving in - even in St Agnes.*"

Fortunately for us not a lot has changed since this article was written thirty five years ago, subsequent owners have kept the traditional feel of the bakery and the lovely smells still greet you in the pre-dawn hours. For the last twenty years the bakery has been run by Mike and Sue Amor.

time, once the Fire Brigade had been informed, a Bugle-boy had to ride around Redruth on horseback alerting the firemen. "*In the meantime the horses had been taken from Tabb's Hotel to the fire station at Falmouth Road and harnessed up to the engine and tender. The firemen arrived, lit the fire to get up steam and complete with brass helmets mounted the horse-drawn machine and galloped to the fire.*" Is it any wonder the bakery burnt to the ground?

By 1920 William Henry Cowl owned the bakery and it remained in the Cowl family until 1979.

On the 23rd May 1928 the R C G carried the

left Mr Cowl's delivery wagon which simply has the word "*Bakery*" on its side. Was this the vehicle involved in the accident at Silverwell?

Shops at the Top of Town Hill

The photographer took this view in 1914 to capture the St Agnes Wesleyan Sunday school tea-treat as they paraded through the village. In the background he has captured four interesting shops. On the left is a drapery shop run by Mrs Nancy James and her two daughters, perhaps it's them standing outside the shop. Next on the right is the bakery with a delivery wagon by the front doors. The building adjoining the road with the small-pane window was at this time a separate shop to the bakery; it was a butcher's run by John Pearce. It later became a fish and chip shop and after the Second World War it was incorporated into the bakery.

On the far right is one of the two lock-up shops that stood where the seats at the top of Town Hill are today. One was a newspaper and fancy goods shop run by Miss Mary Sloggett. On the 21st June 1906 the Royal Cornwall Gazette reported, *"Visitors may be glad to know that the London dailies may be had at Miss Sloggett's Newsagents Churchtown and that the Royal Cornwall Gazette, the principle county paper may be had there about noon on Thursday"*.

A year earlier, on the 10th August 1905, the R C G said, *"For the convenience of visitors it may well be noted that a lending library has been established by Miss Sloggett, Churchtown, St Agnes - the District Agent for the Royal Cornwall Gazette"*.

The second shop adjoining this one but out of view was a cobbler's run by Joseph Quick.

right The top of Town Hill on a snowy day. The railings on the Church wall date this photo as pre Second World War. The lock-up shops have long since disappeared.

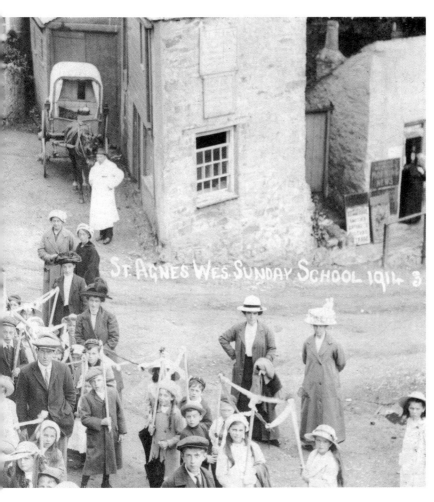

left This photograph was made into a postcard and has the strange message on the back, *"Dear Flo, our tea-treat. I must have eaten well, note what a barge I look. Nance"*.

ST. AGNES WES. SUNDAY SCHOOL 1914

below John Pearce with his butcher's wagon in the entrance to the Vicarage c. 1900.

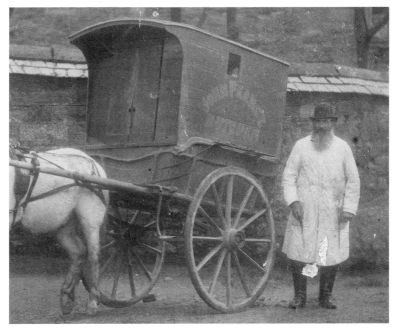

Town Hill

right Two ladies in long dresses and smart hats push their bicycles up Town Hill c. 1910. A little girl pauses for a chance to be included in the photograph.

On the left are nine stepped cottages - Stippy Stappy. These were built around 1840 and owned by the Hitchens family who managed the harbour at Trevaunance Cove. Many of the tenants of these cottages were ship's captains or sailors.

right Two-way traffic in Town Hill c. 1960. Even today it is not entirely a thing of the past with many summer visitors mistakenly trying to drive the wrong way.

left Town Hill in the early 1920s.

left Town Hill and Stippy Stappy from Wheal Kitty in 1905.

Acknowledgements

I would like to express my sincere thanks to everyone who helped me with this book. It has been a pleasure to compile and much of this is due to the help and kindness of the people who provided me with photographs and information:

Mike & Sue Amor, Mike & Ann Bunt, Allan & Hilda Butler, Roy Castine, Percy Cheesley, John Dale, David & Wendy Docking, John Down, Paul Kimberly, George Kimmins, Roger Lacy, Margaret Leadbeatter, Douglas Mitchell, Christopher Morrison, John Murrish, Anthony Paul, Roger Radcliffe, Billy Roberts, Betty Russell, Alan Thomas, Peter (Nick) Thomas, Tom & Liz Thompson, Claude & Betty Tonkin, Betty Tredinnick, Brian Trickett, Keith & Val Woolcott, Cyril & Dawn Woon and Ken Young.

I have made every attempt to trace individual photographers but in some instances this proved impossible. I hope that any I couldn't find will accept my apologies and understand that no photograph has been included without extensive efforts to identify who took it and to obtain approval for its inclusion.

My research has been greatly helped by the excellent staff of the Courtney Library at the Royal Institution of Cornwall, the Cornwall Centre and the County Record Office; these are invaluable sources of information for local historians.

I would especially like to thank Tony Mansell and Alan Murton. Tony has spent many hours reading the text and advising me during the book's production and Alan has completed the final proof reading. Finally I would like to thank my son Daniel for his design and typesetting skills.

References

The Story of a Village Street by Frank Carpenter
Victorian Redruth by Michael Tangye
Cornwall's Fire Brigades by Ivan Rabey
Views and Likenesses by Charles Thomas
The Parish of St Agnes by Thomas Tonkin (Journal of the Royal Institution of Cornwall 1975/6)
St Agnes Official Guide 1925
Various St Agnes guides
The Women's Institute Album 1951
Miners and Mechanics' Institute Centenary Booklet
Little Puppet Theatre programme
St Agnes Church magazines
Board Of Highways minutes 1841 - 1863
Royal Cornwall Gazette Newspapers (Courtney Library, R.I.C. Truro)
West Briton Newspapers
Down your way August 1970 on tape (St Agnes Museum)
Kellys and other trade directories (Cornwall Centre, Redruth)
Tom Thompson interview notes
Eddie Tredinnick talk 1970 (St Agnes Museum)
Alf Bunt interviewed on tape by Frank Carpenter in 1983 (St Agnes Museum)
The Journal of St Agnes Museum Trust;
    No. 1 Editorial by Roger Radcliffe
    No. 4 White Hart Hotel by Frank Carpenter
    No. 5 St Agnes Posts by Bill Morrison

Books by the same author
    St Agnes Parish 1850 - 1920 A Photographic Record (1986)
    St Agnes Parish 1920 - 1950 A Photographic Record (1988)
    Around St Agnes - The Archive Photographic Series (1996)
    St Agnes - A Photographic History. Volume One - Down Quay (2005)

Books by the same author with Tony Mansell
    A History of Blackwater and its Neighbours (2004)
    Jericho to Cligga, Trevellas and Crosscoombe (2006)